Shooting Stars

Kirstie Cheree Williams

Presentation by *BookLeaf Publishing*

Web: www.bookleafpub.com

E-mail: info@bookleafpub.com

ISBN: 9789358368574

First edition 2023

*I dedicate this book to my son Angel and my
brother Brittney. I love you both to the moon
and back!*

ACKNOWLEDGEMENT

Thank you Bookleaf Publishing for this writing opportunity.

I'd like to acknowledge Lydia Nickleberry, for sponsoring me to take on this writing challenge.

PREFACE

When the world spins

It seems like there is nothing you can do. You feel like you're drowning, where everything is surrounding you and you can't breath. I absolutely hate that feeling. It's awful! But I think I cracked the code. Or at least found a code the escape room we call "life".
I am so tired of feeling down and sad. And although I've never been clinically diagnosed as depressed, I definitely feel like I am. After losing people that you love, how can you feel like yourself again? You are forever changed.

I wanted to feel better. I even started therapy. I dove into the world of self care. In 2020 during the pandemic I convinced myself I had to make a change in order to feel like somebody again. Losing a child changed me, and I will always grieve my baby boy. And as I learned about inner child healing it help me to overcome a lot of the heartbreak. I started to slowly piece myself back together, my boyfriend and I moved out of the city for a fresh start, and I decided to finally do the things I once loved. My boyfriend and I call it our self care routines. I wanted to do the things I once loved, so I try to stay active in a hobby. I got into makeup and skincare videos. Ways to look fashionable, claiming you will feel beautiful. And you know what?

I had fun! It was such an amazing experience to finally buy a few nice things and do a few nice things for myself. It's become a bit of a habit, I must admit.

Even though I was keeping up on my routine, I still found myself sad more than I feel like is considered "normal". And just recently my brother died. It is all so fresh in my mind that I get emotional almost everyday. But I would tell myself every single day, I don't want to be sad.

As I was ending a crying session the answer just hit me. Taking care of my mental state is a huge part of self care. Although most articles start with: "when we hear self care we think about warm bubble baths, spa treatments, and taking yourself out on a date". I only recently understand that taking care of your brain is just as important. Mental health is a huge part of taking care of yourself, because how you feel is how you operate, and your body will not be able to enjoy those cucumbers over your eyes and that mud bath because your mind will constantly be elsewhere.

It kills me that I lost a major part of me. Well, not really lost but there is part a can't access currently. I think this life chapter is about me trying to find myself again. Finding the me that I want to be. I am not certain if I will ever find that missing side of me. But I can start by taking care of my mental health. I really hope that this collection of poetry comes across clear and easy to understand. They were written during moments of grief, and an are a special part of my healing.

I'd Give Anything in This World to Hold You Again

I am so grateful to have held you.
I will never forget how you felt.
You were so small, and fragile.
Your skin was so soft.
I could feel your tiny skull when I just ever so
gently caressed the top of your head.
And it was so smooth as I placed my nose on
your face to smell and kiss you.
I could feel your tiny rib cage as I gently ran my
finger down your chest.
I could scoop your small hand around my
fingertip.
And your foot was so small could fit perfectly
against the pad of my finger.
I would give anything in this world just to touch
you again.
To lift you up was like lifting air.
Your body was cold as ice.
I would give anything in this world to hold you
again.
At least I hold you in my heart.

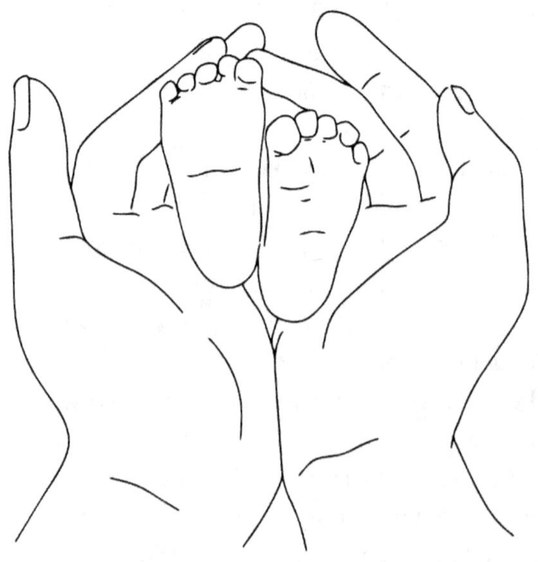

Baby Steps

I tried to be social today.
I went out and about.
Ran a few errands before going to an event.
And it was nice.
People were thriving.
People were smiling.
And I wanted to have fun too.
I tried, for you.
But no matter what I did or said
I continued to feel like I was left on read.
And I wanted to stop because I was left on red
But I continued on
Because I wanted to go.
I wanted to do this.
Stepping out of my comfort zone
and into the crowd.
Attempting to maintain my composure
Though the screams are loud.
Afterwards I sat in the car.
I took time for myself but I didn't cry.
I guess I should be proud
Because for you I tried.
It's baby steps.

Unplug

I'm at a point where I really want to unplug.
But it's a really hard and deep hole I dug…
I got in this mess when I lost a piece of my
heart.
And now I feel like I need to hit restart.
I grieve everything I never got to do.
Pictures, feeding, holding, loving, and simply
raising you…
Birthday coming up again and this time you'll
be two.
It hasn't gotten easier. The grieving only grew.
I'm always on my phone scrolling my life away.
Wasting time with nothing to show, just lazy
everyday.
I watch TV and play the game so I don't have to
think.
Because I don't like the sensation of feeling my
heart sink.
My mind is literally gone as my eyes stare at the
screen.
Hiding my true feelings because I don't want
them to be seen.
I need to put my phone away and turn the tv off,
And rest my eyes and brain and breathe,
vulnerable and soft.

I gotta unplug and look in the mirror and find
myself again. I'm not ready to give up or let this
be the end.
I want when you watch over me for you to feel
so proud.
Sometimes it's hard because I just don't feel you
are right now.
But I promise you this through these painful
moments, I will try
To unplug and focus on myself, even if I cry.

Broken

I am broken. Who knew that the heart was so fragile? Jesus is close to the broken hearted... That's what they say. I hope He is close to me. Because I feel so alone. I'm starting to think my heart is not strong enough for the heartbreaks of earth. I think I'm better off alone. Nothing is new under the sun. History repeats. People are constantly alone. I am not by myself.

Suffering in Silence

Put on your mask.
It happens every so often.
And it stings when it does.
Heart drops. Eyes burn.
Screaming inside your head.
Screaming with no one to hear your cries for
help.
Suffering in silence.
Feeling pain being inflicted, but no bruises
appear.
Pick up the mask.
It's heavy.
Put it on and pretend to be anything other than
yourself.
You want to escape but there is no where to go.
You try to tell yourself to stop the sabotage.
You are so used to it, it's in you now, it is you
now.
Walking this big wide earth.
Trying to find purpose.
The pain slows you down.
Because it hurts.
And you try to wear the mask.
And keep pushing. Still moving.
No one can see your scars.

Who even wants to?
You don't want sympathy!
Just a friend.
But the neglect chases.
No matter the places you go or the things you
do.
There's no respect for you.
You can't even help yourself.
Even though you try to.
But you never know when you're being lied to.
Put on your mask.
Try to cope with the hope that something good is
coming your way.
Work like ants.
There seems to be no purpose in anything
anyway.
Keep moving forward until you fizzle out.
Eventually you will burn up like a shooting star.
Doubts fill your mind.
Fear fills your heart.
And I know you want to let all of this go
But there's no where to put it.

So put on your mask.

My Baby is in Heaven

My baby is in heaven.
In such a special place.
I see his little smile
When I think about his face.

He sends me signs in dragonflies,
In clouds, and numbers too.
He sends me these to comfort me,
When mommy's feeling blue.

My baby is in heaven
Where the Angel babies go.
An angel baby nursery
With cribs all in a row.

Baby seats and bouncers,
Balloons, bubbles, balls.
Our families and ancestors
are there to watch them all

My baby is in heaven.
And although we're far apart.
He's always on my mind.
And he's always in my heart.

I Need You

Oh how sad I feel!
You are so important to me.
And I'm not sure if I'm am empath,
But I feel as though I cannot function
When you are sick.
I feel weak.
Like a part of me isn't functioning right,
My joints are not as fluid as they used to be.
I already think so slow and my mind cannot
keep up.
It's hard for me to see, up.
Up up and away!
Upward towards positivity and peace.
And being able to carryon in grace.
When I look in the mirror and see my face.
The tears in my eyes.
The pain in my heart.
My soul cries out!
I want to be loved!
I want to be heard!
My soul cries out.
Don't leave me alone.
Please get better.

I need you.

Don't Stop (haiku)

The show must go on.
The Earth will just keep spinning.
Time waits for no man.

Until You Go Through It

I can't seem to find the words I want to say.
If you were to ask me right now, no I'm not
okay.
I write everyday, meditate and pray that
eventually I can get my happiness to stay.

I'm anxious about life and doing adult things.
I worry the healing process may not work for
me.
I'm scared to lose all the others to whom I've
given a heart piece.
I fear that I won't be able to hear another heart
beat.

When I'm by myself, it's a safe space.
A bubble that I've created, a total safe place.
Filled with good thoughts I'm constantly trying
to chase,
But I can't escape with the bad thoughts always
on my case.

Why is it easier to write when I'm in pain?
Why do the words flow when you have nothing
for which to gain?

Why? Why is life so hard to figure out and understand?
Why won't these negative feelings just leave my head?

I don't know if you'll fully get it.
Unless you've gone through it.

Incomplete

I still feel incomplete.
I hoped after this I would feel better.
Like things would be okay somehow.
But they're not.
I still have to work.
And eat.
And survive.
But I don't know how!
Sometimes
When I sit and it's quiet and I'm all alone
That's when it comes for me.
The bad thoughts that plague my mind.
I want to hide.
It's too scary to live boldly.
I don't know what's out there.
I don't know when it's gonna come for me.
And none of it feels real anymore.
I just feel incomplete.

Anxiety

I'm torturing myself by being afraid to go to
sleep at night.
Not knowing what the day will bring.
Will it bring joy and sunshine?
Or sadness and rain.
Im having those anxiety attacks again.
Im grateful that I can recognize it.
I guess that's baby steps again.
But that's only half the battle.
I want to go out and do fun things,
And try new fun things and meet new people.
If I did that,
I bet I could change my whole life!
But I'm too afraid to do that,
Because it could change my whole life.
And so I sit here too lazy to move
And it's all because of fear?
I'm sorry but,
I don't know what to do with that information.
I'm supposed to just figure out, on my own,
Just know how to navigate this world?
That's absolutely and totally unfair!
Why can't it just be easy?
This pain hurts.
And I don't know where I am supposed to put it.

I don't know what to do with it.
I'm too scared.

Joy Comes in the Morning

I'm going to miss your laugh.
Our inside jokes were real.
This has happened way to fast
I don't know how to heal.
I know that time should heal all wounds
But this just cut too deep.
You said you don't believe in God,
Yet I pray your soul, He keeps.
Your smile was worth a thousand words,
Your eyes, they shone so bright.
You could move mountains with your words
Your arms could hug so tight.
Gentle as a feather,
Bold as bold can be.
You'll always be my brother.
Forever can't you see?
I do not have to be afraid.
I know that you are near.
As joy comes in the morning!
I shall not live in fear.
I shall not be alone.
So now the work begins.
I can make it through this.
The devil will not win.
It might be raining now,

My heart is filled with sorrow.
But I stand tall because I know
The sun gone' shine tomorrow.

Rain

Rain rain go away.
The cold and fleeting breath escape.
The moon beams across the waters.
You are now safe my love.
Rain rain go away!
Child sing your song.
The blue will melt away.
You are free to live and play.
Find the beautiful things,
The glistening jewel,
The sounding bird,
The air on your face.
Rain rain go away!
Sing your song.
The memories hit like hail
The sadness might swell
The tears begin to fall.
But when they do, stand up tall.
Stand up tall and sing your song.
For you are safe, my love.
Safe to be your truest self
It's okay to be vulnerable.
Sing your song my love.
Rain rain go away.

Friends

Sometimes you gotta phone a friend.
It's more than a distraction.
A friend who will lend their time,
A word, or an action.

To have support means many things.
It's something we all need.
Someone to believe in you.
And to help you sow a seed.

To lift you up when you're faced with dispair.
To push you past your limits.
To remind you not to give up and quit.
To encourage you to win it.

A friend is needed to take your hand.
When you are feeling weak.
A friend to help you take a stand.
Someone who's unique.

It's hard to get by when you feel like there's no
one in your corner.
You might think you're all alone, in this world a
foreigner.

I leave this message for anyone who feels
somewhat like me.
Someone out there understands,
For history repeats.

A friend, a group, or therapy
Seek out what works for you.
You're not in this alone!
I know this to be true.

So when you feel the grief return,
And sadness wells inside
Think about who's in your life,
Find a friend you can confide.

Neglect

I forgot to water my plants.
I can't remember when the last time was that I
watered them.
But one day, I came out my bedroom and
realized...
I completely neglected my plants.
I sat in disbelief.
I was doing so good keeping them alive, for
someone who doesn't have a green thumb.
But I forgot to water them.
By now, the leaves are yellow.
I must forgive myself.

What else have I neglected?

Family

When someone dies it makes you cling to
family.

Grief forces you to open up your eyes and see
That the only thing that matters in this would is
You and me.

You and me.
We can survive this.
We will get through this.
Somehow.

I can't do this by myself.
I've cried everyday since.
Someone please make it make sense!

I'm grieving and it hurts.
Brother, sister, stand by me.
I will stand by you too because I know you have
pain. We all do.

We must cling to one another
Now more than ever.
The only thing that matters in this world is you
and me.

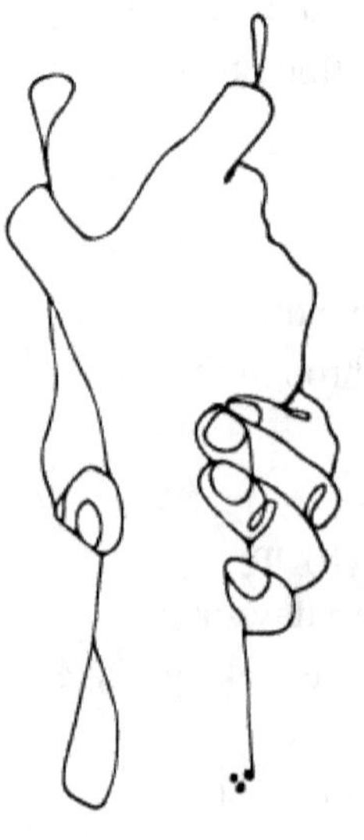

Denial and Anger

This still does not feel real.
No way no chance in hell.
He was just here.
We just talked.
I heard his voice.
I felt his presence.
And as I go on,
I still can't believe this.
We celebrated his life.
We shared memories of him
And I'm supposed to just accept the fact that he's
gone?
I'll never see him again?
Why didn't he see a doctor?
Why did he let this go on for so long?
This should not of happened this way!
He deserved better.
He deserved more.
He had ideas.
He had dreams and goals.
But now he is just a memory.
I'm so pissed.
Why did this happen?
How?
And no one can explain.

These feelings building up inside.
I'm going to explode.
I don't know where to put these emotions.

Bargaining and Depression

When we got the news,
I didn't want it to be true.
This can't happen to us.
Why did this happen to you?

This is the stage that I dip into most.
Like a lump on a log I lay.
The sun has already set.
You mean I missed a day?

Kitchen bathroom bedroom.
Household upside down.
I think that I've stepped out of it.
I just get turned around.

Tears fall til the well is dry.
Throat burns from the screams.
You know it's bad when someone asks
"Hey, did you eat?"

Stars give me comfort
Their twinkling light gives hope.
It maybe just a glimmer.
Or just the way I cope.

Eventually I return to bed.
Just the way I started.
To dwell upon my close kin.
My dearly departed.

Acceptance

Acceptance means it's OK to laugh
Even though you have passed
I can still find joy
I know that you are always near me
You would want me to live on
You would want me explore
You would want me to try new things
I am still blessed
And there is so much of the world to see
The world feels a little bit lighter
But that's OK
I know in my heart
I will see you again one day
And until that day comes
I will do my best
To be grateful for each day
And never ever take a moment for granted.
I want to be present in every moment
I want every moment to bring new meaning to
my life
I have to find acceptance
So that I can live my life
It's hard
So hard
But I know I'll be OK
I can do this

I Am Alright

I want to tell you what comes next
But to be honest
I am not sure
I want to say that she will love happily ever after
But I don't think that's how it works
I think we are just meant to observe every
moment
And take everything in
And not rush and worry about tomorrow.
I think every minute I should focus on the
present. And be grateful for every beautiful
thing that God has placed here
I am alright
I can release all the tension
Negative bound so tight
I release you from my body
Flee from my soul.
You will never have me
I am safe
And I am loved
Beauty surrounds me
So does peace
I am alright

Angel's Story

One very gloomy day I was having a sad moment because I was missing my son. I was expecting my first child and back in May of 2020, I underwent an extremely traumatic experience. I developed a pain in the lower right quadrant of my body that had become so great, I felt that I needed to see a doctor. When I went, they didn't find anything wrong and sent me home. The pain never went away and I went back two days later because I began to have contractions. When I got to the hospital my water broke as soon as I walked through the emergency doors and a short time later, my baby was born and there was nothing that could be done to save him. I had just made it to 18 weeks gestation. None of the doctors could explain why this had happened to me.

My whole life changed in that moment. The once bubbly and happy-go-lucky girl was gone. I became an extremely anxious person and although I was never diagnosed, I believe I suffered from postpartum depression. I couldn't find the strength to believe, to love, and I definitely didn't have any peace. Sleeping was a struggle as well. I didn't want to create and I was completely uninspired to do anything. Someone who was once so imaginative and optimistic had lost all hope.

I would put on my best mask for everyone, pretending to be happy while suffering in silence. It wasn't until I was around my parents that I felt a glimmer of hope again. Being around my them when I needed them most was a healing experience. They became a source of energy for me. And they gave me the courage to know that everything would be okay.

I took therapy and leaned on God so much that I was able to take more steps towards healing, and eventually I was able to become my own light again. I believe that it is so important to be surrounded by those you love when you are down and out, and sometimes you have to be your own light. I am most active when the sun is out, and I am so grateful for the fiery energy it provides. I want to shine my light on others and inspire others to not give up. I want to be able to encourage others as my parents have encouraged me when I was down. It is only through the light that they shone on me that I was able to reignite my own fire within, and I have to share that with the world.

I feel like my son is with me, pushing me to continue and live in with strength. And I know that I will make it through.

37

www.ingramcontent.com/pod-product-compliance
Lightning Source LLC
LaVergne TN
LVHW021312200726
843509LV00012B/1890